# How to budget with your Pocket money

**Annie Chisambo**

DORMOUSE

© Annie Chisambo 2012

Published in the United Kingdom
by Dormouse Press, an imprint of
Guidemark Publishing Limited.

ISBN 978-0-9569466-7-6

**www.dormousepress.co.uk**

# What do you do with your Pocket Money?

**Do you save it? Share it? Or spend it?**

Why not try to do all three - save, share and spend? It's tempting to spend all of your money, but it's better to save some too. It's also good to share a little of your money, if you can.

This book will show you how to plan your spending, manage a budget and keep track of what you save, share and spend. Learning how to budget with your pocket money NOW will help you manage your money in the future when you start work and begin to earn wages. It will also help you avoid debt. **Let's get started!**

# What is a budget?

**A _budget_ is:**

An amount of money set aside for something

**It's also:**

A plan you make with your money (that's what this book is about)

## The Golden Rule:

You can't spend more than you have!

## TOP TIP

As you read through this book, you'll see that some words are shown in bold and underlined (**_like this_**). You can find out what these words mean by turning to the glossary on page 24.

## MOO-NEY FACT

Cattle have been used as a form of money for a long time. Cattle were used as cash as far back as 9000 BC. In parts of Africa they were still being used as money as recently as the middle of the 20th century.

# Why should you budget?

## It puts you in control of your money

Take the time to decide what you want to do with your money. Don't go on a spending spree every time you receive some cash. Try to:

- Save a certain amount.
- Share or give some of your money to help others.
- Get the best price when you buy.

## Budgeting helps you avoid getting into debt

**_Debt_** is money that you've borrowed and need to pay back. If you manage your money well, you will be less likely to get into debt. Budgeting also helps you plan how to pay back what you owe.

## Keeping a record of your budget

Every time you receive or earn money, make a plan. To keep a record of your money you'll need:

- Some PAPER and a PEN, or use a COMPUTER
- A CALCULATOR
- A FOLDER or FILE (for your plan) or use a large NOTEBOOK

# A budget helps you to understand where your money is going

Once you know what you're spending your money on, you can easily make changes if you want to achieve a savings goal. For example, if you want to save £12 and you know that you spend £4 a week on sweets, you can:

**Decide not to eat sweets for three weeks.**

(3 x £4 saved = £12)

**Or eat fewer sweets for a while. For example, you could reduce the amount you spend on sweets to £2 for six weeks.**

(6 x £2 saved = £12)

# Income (money coming in)

**Income** means the money you receive. Your income is your pocket money and any money you earn from doing chores, or a job such as a paper round.

## Pocket money

Not everyone gets pocket money but, if you do, it's time to start budgeting. It's not smart to spend it all.

## Quick Quiz

On average, how much pocket money do children in the UK get each week?

A. £4.44 a week
B. £5.89 a week
C. £6.25 a week
D. £8.37 a week

You'll find the answer at the bottom of this page.

Source: Halifax Children's Pocket Money Survey

## BIRTHDAY CASH

If you're given cash for your birthday, you may be tempted to spend it all. Always remember that some of the cash may come in useful in the future, so it's wise to save some of it.

## TOP TIP

If you know someone is going to give you money for your birthday, ask them to give you a **cheque** (if possible) instead of cash. You will have to take the cheque to the bank and so will be less likely to spend it.

Answer: C - £6.25 a week

# Cheques

A ***cheque*** is a written instruction telling your bank to pay someone. It looks like this:

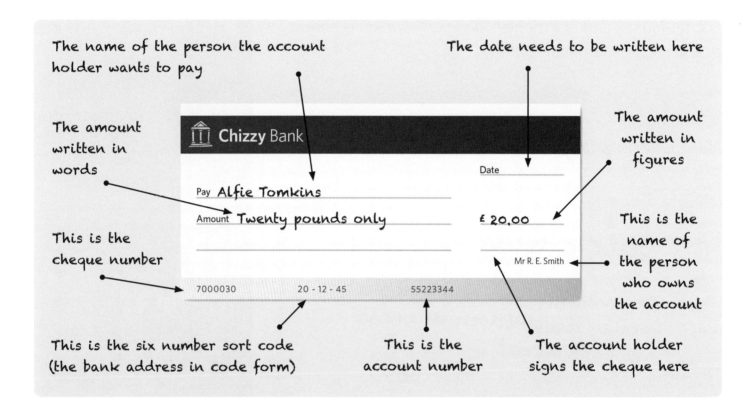

The name of the person the account holder wants to pay

The date needs to be written here

The amount written in words

The amount written in figures

This is the cheque number

This is the name of the person who owns the account

This is the six number sort code (the bank address in code form)

This is the account number

The account holder signs the cheque here

**Chizzy** Bank

Date

Pay Alfie Tomkins

Amount Twenty pounds only

£ 20.00

Mr R. E. Smith

7000030          20 - 12 - 45          55223344

Fewer cheques are being written every year because more and more people are now paying for things using a ***debit card***.

A debit card is a plastic card that adults use to draw money from their bank account. They can also use it to pay for the things they buy in shops or online. To stop other people using the card, the cardholder has a secret ***PIN*** number that only they know.

# Your first budget

Let's pretend that last week you received £10 pocket money and earned £5 from doing chores, which means your total *__income__* was £15. You had no money left over from the previous week. Go to **www.yourpocketmoney.co.uk** to download a blank budget sheet and write down your income from last week. **This is how it should look:**

|  | Money In | Money Out | Balance |
|---|---|---|---|
| Pocket money | £10.00 | - | £10.00 |
| Chores | £5.00 | - | £15.00 |

The *__balance__* column shows the amount of money you have at any particular time.

**Help around the house - don't be lazy, be creative!**

To earn extra money, ask your parents or carers if they would be willing to pay you to do chores around the house.

YOU COULD:

Walk the dog (if you have one)
Load the washing machine
Water the plants
Empty the bins
Wash the dishes

... what other jobs can you think of?

# Save, share and spend

**Now that you have some money, it's time to decide what you will do with it. Here are three good reasons to save money:**

## Save for the future

Tuition fees are £9,000 a year at most universities, and they may be even higher by the time you're old enough to go. That's why it's a good idea to start saving now. As you get older, the kind of things you choose to save for will change. When you leave home you may want to save for a holiday, a car, or for a **_deposit_** on a house. Eventually you may also want to save for your **_retirement_**.

## For an expensive item
Save up to buy things like a bike, guitar or a computer.

## It's sensible
If your money is in the bank, you'll be less tempted to spend it on things you don't need. It's also useful to have some money in your account in case something unexpected happens.

## SAVING YOUR MONEY
When you save money you'll have less cash to spend now, but you will have a lot more to spend in the future.

# Saving your money

**The safest place to keep your money is in the bank.**

Banks have good security systems and they also give you a little extra money as a "thank you" for saving with them. This is called **_interest_** and it is yours to keep.

The amount of interest the bank will pay you is shown as a percentage, like 3% **_AER_**. This means that for every £100 you save with the bank in a year, they will give you £3 in interest.

## What is AER?

AER stands for Annual Equivalent Rate. The higher the AER, the more interest you will receive.

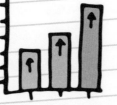

# The £1 challenge

If you saved **£1 a day** with the bank every year from the age of 18 to the age of 60, here's how much you'd end up with, based on different interest rates:

| | | | |
|---|---|---|---|
| 1% AER £19,125 | 2% AER £24,148 | 3% AER £30,837 | 4% AER £39,790 |
| 5% AER £51,828 | 6% AER £68,075 | 7% AER £90,073 | 8% AER £119,933 |

If you left the money in a piggy bank at home, you'd only have £15,330.

> "You can have an account at any age. As soon as you are born and have been given a name, your parents can open a savings account for you. They can use the account to start putting money away for your future."

A bank account is where your money is held. You can open as many savings accounts with as many banks as you like.

# Opening a bank account

To find the best savings **_account_** use a website that compares the different banks. It's a good idea to get help from an adult to compare account features to make sure you find the best deal.

## Features

- How much interest will you get?
- How often can you take your money out?
- How much will you need to open the account?

**To open an account, your parent or carer will need to:**

**1.** Ring the bank to make an appointment for you both.

**2.** Take your birth certificate or a passport along when you go to the bank. You will also need to take a **_utility bill_** such as a gas, electricity or water bill.

**3.** Make the first **_deposit_** – in other words, pay some money into your account. This can usually be as little as £1.

Remember: **saving a little every month will eventually add up to a lot!**

### Why does the bank need to see a utility bill?

The bill will have the name of your parent or carer and your home address on it. This will be used by the bank as proof of where you live. They will also use the address to send you information about your account.

### Can I take out the money whenever I want?

You can usually **_withdraw_** (take out) the money you have saved with the bank when you need it. You will need to get your parent or carer to go to the bank with you until you are 16 or, sometimes, 18 years old.

# Sharing your money

Now that you've managed to save some of your money, the next thing to do is to consider sharing some of it, (but not all of it). Sharing is a lifestyle choice that only you can make.

**Three reasons why it's a good idea to share:**

### To help those in need

It feels good to give to others, either by helping someone who is less fortunate than you, or by buying presents for friends and family. If you'd like to help a charity, go online and search for national and international charities, and those that are local to your area. When you share your money you will have less to spend on yourself, but your generosity will help other people and cheer them up.

### It can make you feel great

Surveys have shown that people who are generous are happier than those who aren't. When we share with others, our joy increases.

### We all need help at some point

You will find that if you are willing to share your money, others are more likely to share with you when YOU need it.

# Spending your money

Ok, you've saved some money and you've shared some. Now it's time to spend some! Another word for spending is **_expenditure_**.

### Write down how you plan to spend your money

This will help you to stay focused. With a written plan, you'll be less tempted to spend money on things you don't want or need.

### If you're buying an expensive item, compare prices first

Let's say you've decided to buy a video game. Go online and visit www.google.co.uk/shopping, type the name of the game you want to buy into the search box, and press enter. The search results will show you a list of places where you can buy the video game, along with prices.

### Before you go shopping, make a list

Write down what you want to buy and how much you want to spend on each item - and don't forget to take the shopping list with you! **If you've set aside £14 for a particular item and you find the price in the shop is £16, you can choose to:**

- buy it, but not buy another item on your list
- try to get it cheaper somewhere else or,
- if you can't get it cheaper, save up and buy it when you have enough money.

Whenever possible, try to use discount and bargain shops. You can often find good quality items at lower prices.

## TOP TIP

Supermarkets place sweets and chocolates by the till to tempt you to buy them. Try not to go shopping when you're hungry, otherwise you could end up buying things that aren't on your list.

### Sizzling hot cash

Did you know that in Japan there's a cash machine that heat presses each bill before they're dispensed? You actually get sterilised cash! How hot is that?

### Don't forget to update your budget

Now that you've paid some money into your savings account, shared some of your money, and spent some, you'll need to update your budget sheet. Take a look at how it should be done on the next page.

# Update your budget sheet

**It's time to update your budget sheet to record:** <u>Your savings</u> - you paid £5 into your account towards your university fees. <u>The money you've shared</u> - your school supported the Children in Need charity and you donated £1. You also bought your little brother, Ben, a comic that cost £1.50. <u>Your spending</u> - you went shopping earlier and spent £2 on a book and £4.50 on music. Here's what your budget will look like:

| Item | Money In | Money Out | Balance |
|------|----------|-----------|---------|
| Pocket money | £10.00 | - | £10.00 |
| Chores | £5.00 | - | £15.00 |
| Savings account | - | £5.00 | £10.00 |
| Children in Need | - | £1.00 | £9.00 |
| Comic for Ben | - | £1.50 | £7.50 |
| Book | - | £2.00 | £5.50 |
| Music | - | £4.50 | £1.00 |

You have £1 left (your ***balance***). You'll need to write this amount on the top line of your next budget sheet. Write 'Balance from last sheet' in the item column and £1 in the balance column. You can see an example of how this should look and download a blank budget sheet from **www.yourpocketmoney.co.uk.**

# Your budget action plan

**1. Always make a budget**

To get you started, go to www.yourpocketmoney.co.uk and download the blank budget sheet. Make some copies and keep them in your budget folder.

**2. Make your plan**

Think about what you would like to do with your money and write it down.

**3. Stick to your plan**

Keep to your budget if you can.

**4. Review your plan**

Compare what you're actually spending against your budget. Do you need to make changes by spending less or making a new plan?

Now that you've learned to budget, you can make a plan. Don't forget to use a budget sheet to keep track of what you save, share and spend every week!

## Things to include in your plan:

- how much money you're going to **SAVE**

- how much money you're going to **SHARE**

- what you're planning to **SPEND** your money on.

## Remember

When you fail to plan, you plan to fail.

# Word search

Before you test yourself on the quiz, try out this wordsearch which contains some of the words we've talked about so far.

| T | D | E | P | O | S | I | T | A | M | Y | D | E | H |
|---|---|---|---|---|---|---|---|---|---|---|---|---|---|
| N | E | L | U | R | N | E | D | L | O | G | F | Q | P |
| U | F | I | Z | N | O | P | S | B | N | R | E | O | S |
| O | M | W | N | K | Y | Y | A | C | E | I | K | E | Y |
| C | J | R | N | M | V | Y | V | T | Y | A | N | N | I |
| C | H | E | Q | U | E | Z | I | U | N | E | J | S | U |
| A | U | T | Y | L | D | R | N | T | O | E | S | B | A |
| X | T | I | M | R | E | W | G | B | G | R | I | A | L |
| P | I | W | O | M | O | N | S | F | N | S | D | L | G |
| Z | L | Z | E | V | D | E | T | S | D | H | E | A | L |
| P | I | N | T | E | R | E | S | T | O | C | R | N | D |
| I | T | S | M | Y | H | B | A | N | K | E | L | C | L |
| P | Y | T | I | S | R | E | V | I | N | U | E | E | R |
| I | S | H | A | L | L | N | X | O | T | F | E | A | Z |

- Retirement
- Utility
- Account
- Interest
- Cheque
- Bank
- Golden Rule
- Deposit
- Savings
- Balance
- Money
- University

If you want to check the answers, go to **www.yourpocketmoney.co.uk.**

# Cash Quiz!

How much do you remember? Try this quiz to find out.

## 1. What is a budget?

A. Money you want to share.
B. Money you have available to spend and a plan you make with your money.
C. Money you want to save.

## 2. What is another word for spend?

A. Pension.
B. Balance.
C. Expenditure.

## 3. What is the golden rule?

A. You can't spend more than you have.
B. You can't spend any of your money.
C. You can't share your money with anyone.

## 4. What is another word for money you receive?

A. Debt.
B. Income.
C. Tax.

5. Where is the best place to keep your money?

A. Under your mattress.
B. With the bank.
C. With your mum or dad.

6. What does "interest" mean?

A. Extra money the bank gives you for saving with them.

B. Extra money the bank takes out of your savings account.

C. Extra money you earn from doing chores.

**Turn to page 23 to check your answers.**

7. Give one good reason why you should budget.

A. So you can show off to your friends.
B. So you know where your money is going.
C. So you can spend all your money.

8. How old do you have to be to have a savings account?

A. 18 or over.
B. You can be any age.
C. 16 or over.

# Crossword

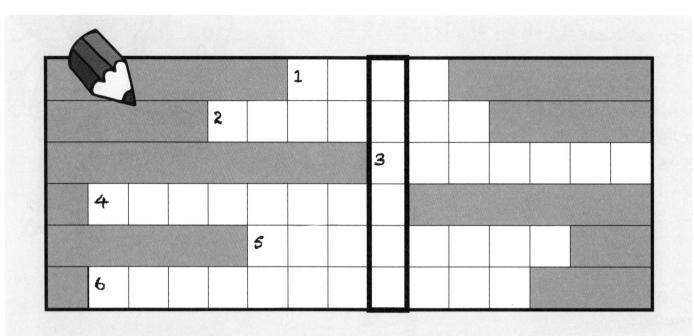

1. Borrowed money that you have to pay back.

2. Holds your money and is provided by the bank.

3. When a person puts money in their bank account.

4. Going to the shop to buy things.

5. The extra money the bank pays you for saving with them.

6. Another word for spending.

# Check your answers

Correct answers to the Quiz
**1B, 2C, 3A, 4B, 5B, 6A, 7B, 8B.**

## How did you score?
**7 - 8** Excellent! You really know your stuff!
**5 - 6** Well done. Just read the questions you got wrong.
**3 - 4** Ok - but you know you can do better.
**0 - 2** Don't be lazy. Read this book again!

Answers to the Crossword

**1** Debt
**2** Account
**3** Deposit
**4** Shopping
**5** Interest
**6** Expenditure

The letters in the box spell **BUDGET**

Ask your parents what they are saving for right now.

Talk to your parents about where their income comes from and how they earn it.

Your parents pay for many things like food, clothes and utility bills. Ask them what other things they have to pay for and what you can do to help them spend less.

# Glossary (what the words mean)

**Account**
This is provided by the bank and is where your money is held.

**AER**
Annual Equivalent Rate, also known as the interest rate.

**Balance**
The amount of money you have left in your account at a particular time.

**Budget**
Either a sum of money you have available to spend, or a plan you make with your money.

**Cheque**
A written instruction telling your bank to pay someone.

**Debit card**
A plastic card provided by the bank. The cardholder can use it to withdraw money from their account or to pay for things they buy in shops or online.

**Debt**
Borrowed money that you have to pay back.

**Deposit**
A deposit can be a payment to secure the purchase of something like a house. It also means money paid into someone's bank account.

**Expenditure**
Another word for spending.

**Income**
The money you receive.

**Interest**
Extra money the bank gives you for saving with them.

**PIN**
PIN is short for Personal Identification Number. PINs are part of the bank's security system. They are secret numbers used as a password to prove that the person who is using the card is the account holder.

**Retire or retirement**
The time after you've given up your job. This is usually around the age of 65, but some people retire earlier.

**Utility bill**
An invoice or bill from a phone, gas, electricity or water company.

**Withdraw**
Take out money that you have saved with the bank.